THE SLEEPING GIANT

THE SLEEPING GIANT

ASHWINI SAHNI and AYLA CANARAN

Copyright © 2018 ASHWINI SAHNI and AYLA CANARAN.

SURAJ PUBLICATIONS
398 WALNUT STREET
646-207-0877
SURAJ PUBLICATIONS

All rights reserved. No part of this book may be reproduced, stored, or transmitted by any means—whether auditory, graphic, mechanical, or electronic—without written permission of the author, except in the case of brief excerpts used in critical articles and reviews. Unauthorized reproduction of any part of this work is illegal and is punishable by law.

ISBN: 978-0-9993471-1-9 (sc)
ISBN: 978-0-9993471-2-6 (e)

Because of the dynamic nature of the Internet, any web addresses or links contained in this book may have changed since publication and may no longer be valid. The views expressed in this work are solely those of the author and do not necessarily reflect the views of the publisher, and the publisher hereby disclaims any responsibility for them.

Any people depicted in stock imagery provided by Getty Images are models,
and such images are being used for illustrative purposes only.
Certain stock imagery © Getty Images.

SURAJ PUBLICATIONS Services rev. date: 03/13/2019

DEDICATION

To my mother, my lifelong teacher

It was the end of summer,
Little Sid walked back one day smiling after school.

He dearly missed the fun days
of playing in the pool!

Mommy asked "How was your day?"

Sid replied : "We laughed, we cried, but we also did play!"

"Teacher asked us to bring a book to class;

She shall select a single, the rest, shall pass!

"She chose a book about a giant (he excitedly screamed with a roar)!

Who found himself shipwrecked ashore,

Trapped by little people called lilliputs;
who nailed him down on the sand with hooks ".

But then the poor little lad
Became sad,
And mad,
Because no one read,
The book he had!

"Sid, why make such a fuss?

Did you know that there is a giant inside each of us?"

"Really? Then the lilliputs are who?"

"The little things that bother you, like irritation, selfishness, greed, laziness, anger and envy too!"

"But mother-
The giant in the book was able to break free!!

But my giant, how can he
Be free, in me?"

Better choices, you shall take,
Better choices, lessen mistakes,
Only then, you will make,
The brave, great giant
Awake."

Sid wondered – "Hmm ....better
choices - how do I get that right ?"

Mom went on ..."Do you remember
the game we played last night ?"

"Yes - snakes and ladder!
I lost it and it made me "madder"

"Ladders are like right choices and will take
you up to the giant and grow your prowess;

Snakes are like wrong choices that
bring you down and leave you helpless"

"Yes mother, I realize now that I am to blame;
when we played the choosing game,

You offered me to choose - candy or a dollar,

I took the candy, if I had made the
smarter choice I could have walked away
with real reward under my collar!

That night, in his sleep;
Sid dreamt a dream so deep;

And saw 'SuperSid' the giant defeat,

The lilliputs who were in retreat!

The next morning, walking to school,

Sid smiled to himself "it's the new me - I rule !

And the giant in me is really cool!"

THE END

The authors created this book to inspire young readers and to remind them that excellence in life is achieved when we "wake up the sleeping giant within each of us" by overcoming our own weaknesses and lower tendencies. Mastery over one's own shortcoming's is the real victory that leads to success in the world!

www.ingramcontent.com/pod-product-compliance
Lightning Source LLC
Chambersburg PA
CBHW060800090426
42736CB00002B/96